MORE PICTURES FROM MY WINDOW

Other books by the author

A WORLD THROUGH MY WINDOW   1978

A PHOTO JOURNAL   1981

RUTH ORKIN

MORE PICTURES FROM MY WINDOW

RIZZOLI
NEW YORK

TECHNICAL NOTE

Film: Kodachrome 64
Filters: None
Tripod: I use a C-clamp with a ball-head instead
Cameras: Contax and Nikon F
Lenses: 20mm to 200mm

Published in the United States of America in 1983 by
RIZZOLI INTERNATIONAL PUBLICATIONS, INC.
712 Fifth Avenue, New York, NY 10019
Copyright © 1983 Ruth Orkin

Library of Congress Cataloging in Publication Data

Orkin, Ruth.
   More pictures from my window.
   1. Photography, Artistic. 2. New York (N.Y.)—
Description—Views. 3. Orkin, Ruth. I. Title.
TR654.O736 1983   779'.997471   82-42846
ISBN 0-8478-0476-3

Designed by Gilda Hannah
Set in type by World Composition Services, Inc., New York City
Printed and bound by Mandarin Offset International, Ltd., Hong Kong

This book is dedicated to:

Frederick Law Olmsted and Calvert Vaux, who in
                1857 had the foresight to build
                Central Park in the first place.

Mimi and Mortimer Levitt, who encouraged me
                at a time when almost no one else
                believed I could publish a book of photographs
                taken from one window.

CONTENTS

PANORAMA FROM MY WINDOW, 1983

Mt. Sinai Hospital

Metropolitan Museum of Art

Adventure playground

Hotel Carlyle

Bandshell

Sheep Meadow

Black tow

Trump Tower

General Motors   Plaza Hotel   Park Lane Hotel

Transverse road

Citicorp   9 West 57 Street

Hotel Pierre   AT&T   Hampshire House   NY Athletic Club   MONY Tower

Ritz Tower   IBM   Tishman Building   Essex House   Sheraton Hotel   Columbus Circle

Tavern-on-the-Green   St. Moritz Hotel   NY Cultural Museum

THE ODYSSEY OF RUTH ORKIN

*To see a World in a Grain of Sand
and a Heaven in a Wild Flower*
William Blake

In the short time since their publication in 1978, the pictures from Ruth Orkin's window of Manhattan's skyline and Olmsted's Central Park have become classics of American photography. This second volume provides stunning, wonderful new evidence of the "window pictures' " unique stature as well as of Orkin's continued growth and maturity as an artist.

Yet, for those familiar with Orkin's earlier achievements as a photojournalist, there was, and continues to be with the publication of this second volume, something perplexing— even disorienting—about her recent pictures (indeed, this was so even for a parks commissioner such as myself who can testify to their uncanny accuracy). The window pictures, no matter how sumptuous, seemed at first glance to discard the very qualities which were the hallmarks of her work in the 1940s and 1950s.

Then, Orkin's taut, black and white vignettes were highly acclaimed staples of the family magazines that thrived in the decades before television completely dominated how Americans saw the world around them. Intelligent, precise, often humorous dramas, her works always seemed to find a human story to tell by looking more closely than the rest of us. She showed us Artur Rubinstein strolling triumphantly through the streets of Manhattan greeting friends and admirers like so many well known musical compositions—warmly, often physically and always with total control. Her photos of a card game among tykes revealed, on second look, a play within a play as each child acted out the antics of some unseen adult model. Carson McCullers seeking the protection of Ethel Water's ample bosom on a perilous opening night; the age-old confrontation between the sexes captured forever, and made sharper by differences in language and culture, as a gauntlet of masculine Italian eyes are held in check by the straight-back stride and upturned chin of an American damsel who has no intention of being in distress; and, of course, yet another portrait of children, this time entranced by the animated story telling of one of their own.

This was the Orkin we knew. Each shot a complete story or the beginning, middle or end of one. That is what she did so well over and over again. Tell stories.

With all that as prologue, what was one to make of Orkin's first volume of pictures from her window overlooking Central Park's Sheep Meadow and Manhattan's skyscraper-chiselled profile? Scenic postcard pictures, of all things, in every conceivable color! The restraint and discipline of her works in black and white suddenly seemed cast aside in favor of sweeping panoramas of sky, nature and those imposing, uniquely American steeples of iron, steel and glass. The human face and posture, an Orkin forte, were no longer close up and sharp, or fixed in compact scenes of theater, but instead were now found sixty-feet below or a seventy-five yards away massed with a hundred or a thousand others.

No matter how perplexing all that was, however, the viewer inevitably put to one side questions about Orkin's apparently quirky artistic odyssey simply to look at the pictures taken from her window. For the pictures, regardless of their origins or the past practices of their creator, were wonderful celebrations of a city and its park, beautiful individually and unexpectedly powerful as a whole.

Still, on the second or third or fourth trip through the window pictures, the mystery of

Orkin's passage inexorably reclaimed one's attention. First a single clue was spotted, then another and at last one saw, as in a festive gathering by Brueghel, a landscape littered with signs of continuity with her artistic past. The window itself was the first clue that the photographer's disciplined intelligence was still intact. Every shot was through the same window, the same frame, the same scene. The pictures from that single point of view were, one came to understand, as strict and as rigorous as a fuque by Bach or a late quartet by Beethoven. The park, the people in it, the buildings and the sky were woven and, in this second volume, rewoven into a complex tapestry of point and counterpoint, theme and variation.

Next it was the light that revealed how close to home Orkin really was all the time (pun, of course, intended). At first it appeared that she had simply walked away from the difficulties of black and white, notwithstanding her obvious mastery of that medium in her earlier work. Perhaps she was no longer up to the challenge. But on closer inspection that concern began to recede as the eye scanned certain winterscapes or returned, for example, to ponder her picture of the Brown Storm. "Are these color shots or not?" you suddenly find yourself asking. The pictures themselves seem to be asking: "what is color or black and white or light and dark?" Questions this fundamental finally lead one to realize just how thoroughly the artist understands both the questions and the answers.

For while Orkin's palette has grown to encompass spring's shattering greens, the bleaching pastels of summer and the hues of autumn, it still retains a special place for the lights and darks of winter. We are not just watching the seasons change. We are watching an artist grow and fill out, responding to a subject as robust and mature as the talent displayed on every page of this book. And still it all begins and ends in black and white,

in color that is there and not there.

The unanticipated power of the window pictures is the final key that unlocks the Orkin mystery. They have an undeniable hold on the viewer. There is a necessity to go back again and again and a need to share them with others. On one occasion there is a sense of sadness and joy. On the next you hear humor and wit, see smiles exchanged and then, from no place you can identify precisely, you feel grief.

What's going on here? What's going on is that Ruth Orkin is doing what she always did best; she's telling stories, staging dramas, with actors both animate and inanimate, with beginnings and ends, plays within plays and plots within plots. And in this second volume the characters are all assembled at center stage for really the first time. In the first book many of the human activities that occurred outside Orkin's window were relegated to an appendix

American Girl in Italy   1951

of black and white photographs. Not so this time; all the actors have been invited into the main hall to embellish and complete the tales first begun in the earlier collection of window pictures.

Look at both volumes together and, of course, it is a history of a city, a nation and, indeed, a world over three decades. The 1960s begin when Castro comes to speak and end with demonstrators chanting for peace; the first Earth Day heralds the arrival of the 1970s, followed by still more gatherings for peace and, finally, a celebration at the war's end; and now the 1980s are upon us as we march to end the arms race.

What gives all this effect, however, are the smaller and less important affairs of humanity and of the city and its people. The Meadow declines and is restored; rugged young men with footballs depart, and sunbathers with blankets arrive. Thousands begin a race with the release of balloons; we see only one finish. The seasons change and sheep dogs replace skiers and skaters and they, in turn, give up their space to modern druids in red robes, Mickey Mouse and five eccentric orange balls. Vendors hawk, Con Edison digs, taxis mate and cops take charge. Concerts and fireworks, marathons and maypoles, sunrise and sunset, even the buildings seem to be alive, creating a skyline as flashy and changing as a crowd at Bloomingdale's. These structures, one begins to feel, are putting on their own parade or, maybe, it's a pageant: showing off, aging

gracefully, suffering untimely deaths, giving unexpected births. And each is a story.

Precisely. It is the oldest of stories—the years go by, the seasons change. Like life, the tale goes on.

All great storybooks and storytellers have certain things in common. From the Old Testament to the fairy tales of Andersen, from Chaucer to Issac Bashevis Singer, each recounts the legends and limits of the human condition, each ponders nature's mutability and the inevitability of change; and, in doing so, they reaffirm the values and truths that have held man and society together throughout history. And so it is with these pictures from a window overlooking a park and a city. Vows of love are exchanged under a canopy of trees. A minstrel is dead and mourners come to share their grief and to honor his life. Yellow streamers celebrate the freedom of hostage prisoners. A tree dies and a meadow is reborn. A violent storm spawns a magic rainbow, a balloon rises, a race is run, the sun breaks through the morning clouds and, transfixed by that beauty, the heart and eye stop.

Ruth Orkin, we learn, has found an altar of life outside her window.

GORDON DAVIS
Commissioner of the Department
of Parks and Recreation
New York City
March 1983

Are They Really All From One Window?

That is the question I've been asked over and over, ever since *A World Through My Window* was published in 1978. The answer, of course, is "Yes!" After my first book was published, people also asked, "Are you going to keep on taking pictures?" Well, the view certainly didn't disappear, so my original reason for shooting still existed.

As I collected the 120 photographs for this book, I realized that what has been happening right here under my window, is a microcosm of what's been happening all over the country:

Demonstrations against war and the nuclear bomb

Memorials for Martin Luther King and John Lennon

Presidents arriving for funerals and campaigns

Buildings coming down—new skyscrapers going up

Parades from the Shriners to the circus

Holidays from New Year's Eve to May Day

Outdoor concerts from Leonard Bernstein to James Taylor

The first New York City Marathon in 1970, and now the whole world runs in it and crosses the finish line directly in front of my window.

Contrary to what could be assumed, I didn't choose this apartment because I wanted to photograph the view. For four years I had been shooting from a second-story brownstone window on West Eighty-eighth Street. I grew very attached to that bay window and the comings and goings of so many people on the street. Now, fifteen stories above Central Park West, everything seemed so far away!

In fact, I wasn't crazy about the immediate view at all. Rather than face the backyard of the Tavern-on-the-Green, I would have preferred something prettier like the Lake around Seventy-third Street. Little did I realize then, that *this* was where the action was. Sheep Meadow, during the sixties and seventies, had supplanted Times Square as the place for happenings, big and small.

So I chose this apartment back in 1955 simply because it was the closest way, in New York City, I could duplicate living on the side of a mountain in Los Angeles—and besides, it was for rent.

View from my window on West Eighty-eighth Street 1952

The view from my window as painted by Mary Orkin   1966

My mother, Mary Orkin with her grandson Andy aged four (left), painting in Central Park on the terrace of the Bethesda Fountain   1963

I think I was destined to have this view. Ever since I was a little girl I wanted to get up on high places so that I could look down and see all those "little" houses and cars and trees. Maybe they looked like toys to me, or the miniature models my father used to build professionally.

Perhaps some four-year-olds are not fascinated by spectacular views of Los Angeles from mountain tops, but I was. Probably because it was instilled in me as my parents drove frequently along Mulholland Drive exclaiming, "Look at that beautiful panoramic view, Ruthie!" "Oh, what a beautiful panomanic view," I chirped back, and mother faithfully recorded "panomanic" in my baby book under "Baby's First Big Words."

Frederick Law Olmsted, one of the builders of Central Park, once wrote about his travels: "While others gravitated to pictures, architecture, Alps, libraries, high life and low life when travelling . . . I had gravitated to parks.

I spent all my spare time in them; when living in London, for instance, and this, with no purpose whatever, except gratification."

The feeling of gratification that Olmsted got from nature and parks, is the same feeling that drove me to high places. I could not arrive in a new city without immediately wanting to make a pilgrimage to its highest point, building or mountain. I had to see the whole place at once to capture that panoramic view. On my bicycle trip to New York City at age seventeen, I went to the tops of the six tallest buildings in the world at that time, before I did any other sightseeing.

As a Californian, I'm still homesick for Los Angeles. Once, when being interviewed for television, the announcer asked, "What draws you to the window?" Knowing that he knew full well what draws me to the window— noise, a change of light, an event, holiday, accident, weather, etc.—I decided to have some fun, thinking that they would of course cut it later.

"Why, nothing draws me to the window! In fact, everytime I look out I wish I could see mountains instead of Fifth Avenue, orange groves instead of Sheep Meadow, and palm trees instead of elms." Well, much to my secret delight, they left it in!

All the years that I've been photographing Central Park from my window, my mother, Mary Orkin, has been doing the same thing— only in oils and from the ground. She was a silent-movie actress when she was young, and didn't pick up a paintbrush until she was sixty-four years old. Today she is eighty-eight.

She paints Central Park exclusively because, as she says, "It's the closest way I can get to the country." She has sold and exhibited her paintings in galleries, and in 1971 *New York* magazine called her "New York City's own Grandma Moses." Her paintings are primitive but reflect a sophisticated style and appreciation of scenic detail and beauty—something that she taught me at an early age.

———————

A few years ago I discovered that I'm not the first photographer to realize that this particular view is unusual. At the turn of the century there were no mass-picture magazines, movies or television. If people wanted to see how the rest of the world lived, they looked at drawings (and some photographs) in magazines or books. Or, they went to a travelogue, which consisted of a lecture plus a slide-show of hand-colored, still photographs, presented by some intrepid adventurer.

Burton Holmes, who lived from 1890 to 1940, was one of the first "Travelogue Men" and it was he who coined the term. In those days a travelogue was the grand event of the season. All over the United States, Holmes played to tuxedo-clad audiences who paid $1.25 to see his presentation, when the latest Hollywood movie cost only a dime.

Shortly after I moved to Central Park West, a friend, Marina Stern, moved into the building that adjoins mine. Her windows are on the same level as mine and just a few yards north. But the inside of her apartment was definitely unique, with twenty-foot-high teak pillars in each corner of the duplex living room. Some ceilings were of ornate Chinese design; one bathroom had black mosaic tile. As I soon learned, it turned out that the former owner was Burton Holmes, and all the unusual decorations were souvenirs from his many travels.

After I'd been shooting from my window for about twenty years, I had some color prints made and began showing them to my neighbors in the building. One day I visited Mrs. Frisch, who lived two floors below me. The minute I showed her the first photograph she said, "Wait a minute! I want you to see something."

Burton Holmes ca. 1940/*New York Times*

"Burton Holmes finds one of the world's most beautiful views from a window of his apartment overlooking Central Park"

She opened a large bureau drawer filled with newspaper clippings. It was a mess! She began rummaging through and came up with a torn, brown clipping of a photograph from the rotogravure section of a 1930s *New York Times.* What a thrill of recognition I felt—it was my view!

Holmes had been asked by the *Times* to select the "Twelve Most Beautiful Places in the World." Along with the Taj Mahal, Angkor Wat and other ancient and modern wonders, Holmes had chosen, as number twelve, "the view from a window of his apartment overlooking Central Park."

———————

Over the years there have been many man-made changes to the view. In almost every instance, I anticipated that the change would hurt my opportunities for taking pictures. In each case, however, I was wrong.

Central Park South in the 1950s

Central Park South and Fifth Avenue
in the 1950s

© Ray Carlson 1977/Joan Kramer & Assoc.

Waiting

After the construction of the black, glass building on East Sixty-seventh Street, I realized that it had ruined the symmetry of the three Con Edison smokestacks. But then I was happy to discover that the black glass was a wonderful relective surface for all sorts of different lighting effects, especially sunsets.

After Warner Leroy reopened the Tavern-on-the-Green in 1976, he discontinued the tradition of the yearly Christmas tree. I was disappointed until I saw the beautiful holiday lights he put up in its place. The lights, all 260,000 of them, are up for six months, from October to March, when they are taken down to allow for the trees to bloom.

When "my" beautiful tree that I'd been photographing for so many years was cut down in 1980, I felt terrible . . . that day. The next day I realized that a brand-new vista into the Meadow had opened up to me.

After Sheep Meadow was resodded and a fence enclosed it, I was afraid there would be nothing more to shoot. That was until the first hot weekend, after it reopened, when I saw the sunbathers stretched out all over the Meadow.

As every new building went up below Fifty-ninth Street, I would envision it throwing the composition, from my angle, out of balance. Instead, each one has settled into the spaces between the older buildings, creating a new composition as aesthetically pleasing as the old one.

As a photojournalist, I never thought of becoming a scenic photographer. The two "window" books are basically long picture stories on one subject. The book that best represents my photojournalism career is in black-and-white and called A *Photo Journal.*

Compared to being a photojournalist, shooting from one window is easy. All you have to do is be there—for years. Then you need the patience to wait until all the elements fall into place: for the right colored car to pass, for the rain to stop, or the parade to start. Also, a photographic eye—I'm frequently reminded—can be helpful.

My only complaint is that it can wreak havoc with appointments, phone calls and other activities, because most scenes and events can't wait until *you're* ready—they require immediate attention. However, I can hardly compare it to the photographically challenging, physically taxing and sometimes dangerous career of being a photojournalist. Those days are behind me, and, now at last, taking care of the "children" doesn't interrupt my shooting anymore. Instead, they interrupt me with, "Hey Mom, look at that cloud out the window." I want to thank the children for helping me shoot the first book—they helped me by keeping me home so much.

In the early fifties I gave up still photography altogether. I had become involved with motion pictures, and became the co-director and co-writer of "Little Fugitive" along with Morris Engel (later my husband) and Ray Ashley. With no previous experience we put together a 35-mm, full-length feature-fiction film that won top prize at the 1953 Venice Film Festival and was nominated for an Oscar. I didn't go on making movies for many reasons, but mainly because there was no Women's Liberation movement around in the fifties to help educate and back me up.

Although my movie-making career was over, I couldn't go back to being a photojournalist—I felt that it would have been beneath me. You can't make thirty-five hundred people laugh in a movie theatre like the Loew's Paradise on a Saturday night, and then feel like taking still-pictures for a living. I had lost interest. If it hadn't been for the view—and also, my wanting to record the children's development—I might never have picked up a camera again.

Then in the late seventies I had my first photographic exhibition at the Witkin Gallery in New York. Now I'm interested in working on more books projects from photographs that I've already taken. Waiting in the wings are Classical Musicians in Rehearsal, Biking Through America in the Thirties, Adventurous Girlhood and more . . . if I can drag myself away from the window.

Richie Andrusco as "The Little Fugitive"   1953

Mary and Andy   1983

CENTRAL PARK—
ITS BEGINNINGS

Most New Yorkers can't imagine New York City without Central Park. What I find difficult to imagine is that it was built in the first place—let alone on such a grand scale. How remarkable that those early New Yorkers had the foresight and the tenacity to propose such a park, especially when the population in 1850 was only 515,000, and most people still lived below Fourteenth Street!

The idea of a park was first inspired by poet/editor William Cullen Bryant, landscape architect Andrew Jackson Downing, novelist Washington Irving and others, who felt that the city should set aside a part of its remaining woodland for the public's future use—before land became too scarce and too expensive. When the city first purchased 684 (later 840) acres of mostly-neglected land in 1851, there were no big city parks in America. In Europe, the public lands had been owned by the nobility and were used by only a small fraction of the population. Inspired by his trips to the great parks of Europe, Frederick Law Olmsted wanted to provide open space for the health, comfort and inspiration of all the city's inhabitants. In 1857 Calvert Vaux, a British-born architect, and Olmsted, a farmer-turned-journalist and a student of English pastoral landscape, won a competition for their plan and design of "Greensward." Together they conceived a plan that eventually turned the middle of Manhattan into a manufactured facsimile of an English landscape.

What Olmsted and Vaux had to work with were swamps, squatter's huts, a dump and other areas described by Olmsted as "filthy, squalid and disgusting." A lot of people think that Central Park was created simply by fencing off the area and calling it a park. Nothing is further from the truth since the park is a totally man-made environment. It may be hard to believe today, but all those hills, lakes, trees, shrubs, pathways and roads were all put there intentionally and painstakingly. The construction became a massive public-works project in 1876 that kept up to four thousand men busy for eighteen years moving earth, rock and water to create what is outside my window today.

Nearly five million plantings were made of 590 species of trees and shrubs and 815 species of flowers and plants. While both Vaux and Olmsted were equally responsible for the general design of the park, it was Vaux who designed the architectural features such as bridges, buildings, fountains and terraces, and Olmstead who administered and supervised the entire operation. The result was an enormous village green set in the middle of Manhattan, and its completion set off a mania of park building across the country.

In addition to some forty public parks in thirty-three states, Olmsted landscaped private estates, college campuses, entire suburbs and even the grounds around Niagara Falls. His work ranged from the capitol grounds in Washington, D.C., to the Stanford University campus in California—from Montreal's Mount Royal Park, to the George Vanderbilt estate in North Carolina. He designed the 1893 Chicago Exposition grounds, which marked the birth of the City Beautiful movement. As the first commissioner of Yosemite Valley (now National) Park in California, his ideas about public land preservation became the philosophical basis for the entire national and state park system.

And that's not all. Olmsted was the first to think and act in terms of suburban design and regional planning; he built the first parkways, along with first coining the word. He is as much the father of American city planning as of the city park. According to William Alex, curator of the Whitney Museum exhibit on Olmsted's 150th anniversary in 1972, "Olmsted is probably responsible for the betterment and preservation of more of the earth's surface than anyone else."

In the last decade, after years of relative obscurity, there has been a surge of interest in Olmsted as our first environmentalist. Three national conferences on Olmsted have been held: in Buffalo, 1980; Boston, 1981 (which I attended); and Chicago, 1982. This year, 1983, the first "World Conference on Olmsted's Parks" will be held September 21–26 in New York City.

CENTRAL PARK 1861

I found the following *Harper's* article* in my library bound in a ragged, antique leather cover. The author, T. Addison Richards, makes the past come alive in his descriptions of the park, the Lake, the ice-skating and his deep appreciation of its meaning to future generations. He shapes the scenes of yesterday with his words, the way Olmsted and Vaux shaped the landscape . . . romantically and picturesquely.

"The long-standing want in the great city of New York of suitable public pleasure-grounds, has within the past two or three years, been amply supplied in the creation of that beautiful Arcadia known as the Central Park; a magnificent domain containing hundreds of broad acres of hill and valley, cliff and copse, lake and lawn, and miles upon miles of winding drives and winning walks, all radiant in a magic atmosphere of art and taste.

"It's dimensions far exceed those of any other pleasure resort yet constructed in the

*From *Harper's New Monthly Magazine*, August 1861

Courtesy of The New-York Historical Society, New York City

Central Park 1857, the year that three hundred dwellings were removed or demolished, along with several factories and numerous "swill-milk" and hog-feeding establishments. Large areas of land, partially covered with stagnant waters, were superficially drained, and ten thousand carloads of loose stone were carried away.

Courtesy of The New-York Historical Society, New York City

View of Central Park from the Ramble looking toward Central Park West on the horizon near Seventy-sixth Street   1860

19

New World . . . also . . . being more than twice the size of either Regent's Park or Hyde Park in London.

"The entire disbursement has reached the liberal figure of some six million of dollars—a large sum indeed, but generously and wisely considered by the people of New York as nothing . . . when compared with the benefits of the enterprise to the public health, pleasure, pride, taste, and morals, for all future time.

"To accomplish this gigantic task, three thousand men set head and heart at work, aided by all the powerful resources of art and science and an unstinte purse. This army of laborers . . . is still busy constructing roads and bridges and arch-ways; turning dreary wastes into grassy lawns, collecting the straggling brooklets into expansive lakes; here leveling the ponderous rock, and there exposing it in more striking and picturesque aspect.

"The Tour, or Drive [East and West] makes the entire circuit of the grounds. . . . It presents a brilliant and inspiring spectable, as seen upon sunny afternoons, when alive with the whirl of a thousand gay and gorgeous carriages, bearing the elite and fashionable of the city through their daily airing.

"The Central Lake is an exquisite reach of bright waters, covering an area of twenty acres, and bounded by a shore of infinite variety and beauty. Upon the upper side are the wooded slopes of the Ramble, stealing down with gentle grassy step, or jutting out in bold, rocky promontory. At the souteast is the grand marble esplanade of the Terrace, with its gorgeous arches, fountains, steps, and statues. At its narrow waist beyond—where it is almost cut in two, like a modern belle—it is spanned by a noble wrought-iron footbridge, with a single arch of eighty-seven and

a half feet. This structure is called the Bow Bridge, from its general likeness in form to a long bow.

"Pretty boats dot the surface of the lake, bearing visitors, for a moderate fee, hither and thither as they list. These little vessels make a winning incident in the scene, especially when filled on summer nights with a ringing chorus of happy hearts and voices. Whole fleets of snow-white swans, too, are ever gliding in stately progress through the winding waters.

"When the ice is in suitable condition, the fact is announced by the elevation of a red ball upon the heights of the Tower Hill, above. The welcome news is immediately repeated by proper signs upon all the cars of the city railways leading to the Park; it is further whispered in the streets, the counting room, and the shops, at firesides and tables, and in boudoirs.

"Every man tells his neighbor feverently that the "Ball is up!" whereupon no matter how cold it may be, all the world, young and old, rich and poor, men and maidens, rush pell-mell to the Park, forthwith put on skates, and hold high saturnalia there from earliest morn to latest night. The winter sport is often shared by as many as ten thousand at the same moment. At the height of the warm season, no less than eighty or ninety thousand people visit the Park daily.

"The surrounding streets and avenues will be graded and paved, and lined with beautiful trees and splendid mansions. . . . Our Park is not for the present day alone, but for all the generations yet to come; and if the generous people of New York shall be remembered and blessed by their posterity for any good deed, above all others, it will be for this inestimable gift."

For a change I'm standing in Sheep Meadow and
shooting toward my window. My apartment
building is the second from the left. ca. 1970

Panoramas

Pink sunset   1981

Sunlit streets in the
east sixties   1977

Strange green mist 1982

Sunrise   1980

Sunset   1980

Evening lights   1980

Evening windows
1962

These five buildings may look as if they're all on
5th Avenue—the Pierre, Sherry Netherland and
General Motors are—but the modern Galleria
and the red-tiled Ritz Tower are on 57th Street
just east of Park Avenue.   1982

Green-cooper roof   1981

Your usual chic New York crowd leaving the
James Taylor concert—67th Street and Central
Park West   1979

Same corner four months later   1979

36

Rally protesting the
Democratic Convention
being held at Madison
Square Garden   1980

Antique-car luncheon   1979

"Caution" 1962

Taxis mating 1979

Three buses filled with the ex-hostages and their families had just gone by. They spent the morning having breakfast at the Tavern-on-the-Green and were on their way to the ticker-tape parade in lower Manhattan. January 30, 1981

Workmen repairing bricks on our building   1982

Right: Movie crew shooting "I'll Cry Tomorrow"
starring Susan Hayward. In those days it was
unusual for Hollywood movies to be shot on
location in New York; today films are shot all
over the city.   ca. 1956

Old Playground. This is the way our old-fashioned playground looked when my children were small. In 1965 Claire Beckhardt and other neighborhood mothers wanted to improve it. At one meeting, which was held in my apartment, we named ourselves "The Committee for a Creative Playground in the Lincoln Square Community." 1963

New Playground. We got such a creative new playground that it attracts parents and children from all over Manhattan. The money was donated by the Estée Lauder Foundation and designed by Richard Datner. 1967

Maypole dancing on the Meadow 1963

Muted autumn   1979

Summer green   1981

Spring on East Drive   1979   Autumn on 67th Street   1978

Winter on the corner of 66th Street and Central
Park West 1981

White feathery trees   1981

A scene from the movie "Kramer vs Kramer" is being filmed in the Meadow. But what this photo also shows is how misshapen "my" tree had become right before it was cut down, and how terribly bare so many spots were on the Meadow right before the resodding.   1978

Right: The brand-new Meadow covered with sunbathers—a view I could never have taken when the tree was there. 1982

Fireworks   1978

Movie lights   1979

Moon over concert
1978

Blue snow
1981

Lighting behind 5th Avenue   1958

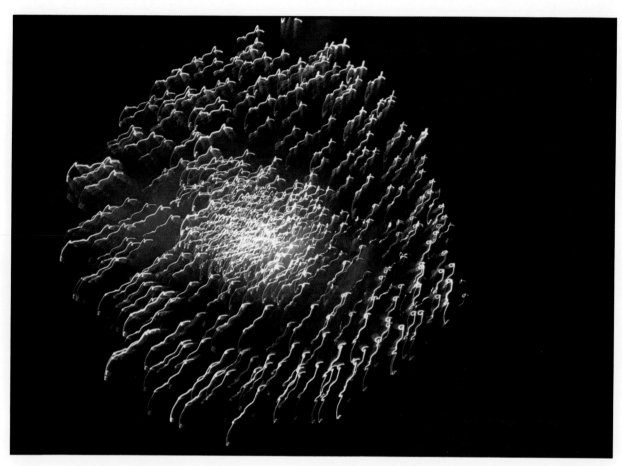

A flower of fireworks   1978

Sheep Meadow lit up for the landing of Nixon's
helicopter in the late fifties

Central Park in preparation for Fidel Castro's
speech in the Bandshell   1959

Yellow blurry lines, the result of a long exposure,
represent people leaving a concert in the Meadow.
There were so many people that they controlled
the flow of traffic and stranded the cars. 1975

This was taken when we could still look through
the Tavern windows and read a menu with high-
powered binoculars. The windows are now
bricked over. The curved, white headlights are
the result of another long exposure.   ca. 1950

Runners on 67th Street. These were all the participants in the first New York City Marathon in 1970, and, with one exception, they were all men. There were 126 starters and 72 finishers. In just twelve years the NYC Marathon went from being an obscure and insignificant race to becoming the world's most prestigious outside of the Olympic Games. In 1982 there were 14,308 starters, including 2,500 women, and 95 percent finished. The runners ranged in age from sixteen to eighty-three and came from sixty-eight countries and fifty states.   1970

Bill Rogers winning the 1979 marathon. The Men's World Record was set in 1969 in Australia by Derek Clayton, and was not broken—even in three Olympics—until Alberto Salazar broke it in the 1981 NYC Marathon. That year I was down at the finish line shooting him from the press bridge. Alison Roe was the women's 1981 winner, also setting a new world record.   1979

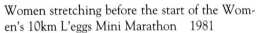

Women stretching before the start of the Women's 10km L'eggs Mini Marathon 1981

Right: The women's mini marathon began in 1972 and today attracts over 6,000 runners. As Grete Waitz has set three world records in the NYC Marathon, she continues to dominate the mini marathon by winning it for the past four years. 1981

Women disappearing
into Central Park at
72nd Street (top of
picture) during the
mini marathon   1982

Winter birds   1978

260,000 holiday lights in front
of the Tavern-on-the-Green 1976

Waiting for the bus   1978

Buried cars   ca. 1960

73

Snowing on 67th Street
and Central Park West
1977

74

During the 1969
blizzard, 6,000 people
were stranded for
three days at Kennedy
Airport. Food supplies
were being airlifted
to the airport by this
police helicopter.   1969

6 p.m. winter 1977

These buildings are barely visible to me anymore
since the trees have grown to block the view.
Also the Heckscher Ball Building, in the fore-
ground, has since burned down. From left to
right is the now-restored Dairy, the Children's
Carousel and the Chess House.   1963

People still ride the bridle paths, though not as often since the 67th Street stables were torn down many years ago, and the American Broadcasting Company was built on the site.   1978

Taxi heading for the tunnel on the 66th Street
transverse   1967

LANDMARK BUILDINGS

Central Park South   1977   The Plaza   1979

Several days out of the year, the sun's angle
makes the Plaza's green-copper roof look like
gold   1976

The Roman window of Temple Emanu-El
at 5th Avenue and 65th Street   1975

Temple Emanu-El surrounded by apartment windows   1982

The Temple in gray haze   1980

Black clouds over
5th Avenue   1981

Double rainbow at sunset 1981

"All's right with the world . . ."

A cult of red-clad people   1981

Top: Herding sheep on Sheep Meadow was done once as a publicity stunt. There were thirty sheep and twelve dogs—each dog was required to herd three sheep at a time into a pen. The Meadow was originally meant to be a grazing place for sheep and was for more than sixty years. The Tavern was their shelter.   1979

Bottom: A "Snow Games" day was held in the Meadow by a local sporting-goods store. There were prizes for the best snow sculpture, and in this scene, determined sports lovers are trying to cross-country ski across the Meadow—on man-made snow.   1979

Sunlovers in March. This hill on the West Drive
frequently becomes a summer-slalom course for
roller-skaters.   1982

Sunbathers in June. The walkers on the West
Drive sidewalk are just finishing a twenty-mile
walkathon.   1982

Resodding fences on an "Irish" meadow. This
race is just one of many held in the park every
year.   1980

One large and one small homemade skating rink
on the Meadow. For seventeen days, skating
enthusiasts came out and kept the rinks cleared.
The little one to the left was for small children.
1977

Baseball during a blizzard!   1979

Cricket players on an English lawn . . . at first
glance . . . turn into frisbee players on the
Meadow   1980

Five orange balloons . . . suddenly materialized out of nowhere. The few sunbathers around seemed unaware of their existence. Sometimes their position changed, but I never saw anybody move them. After a few hours they disappeared as mysteriously as they had appeared. Later I read that their sole purpose was to be photographed—anywhere the photographer chose to set them down.   1981

Ten orange buses . . . waiting for their riders   1961

Golden glow—5th Avenue
and Central Park South   1980

After the rain   1981

July 4th, 1976

Rosy city   1981

Purple city   1981

ANTI-NUKE RALLY
12 JUNE 1982

Left: The huge Anti-Nuclear Rally filled the Great Lawn with an estimated seven hundred thousand to one million demonstrators. The march began in the early morning in front of the United Nations Building, and took exactly three hours to pass under my apartment on Central Park West—and those were less than half. Meanwhile approximately 500,000 others were marching up 5th Avenue for five hours! This was the largest gathering in Central Park—ever.

Right: Japanese marchers

Left: Crowds of mourners for John Lennon gathered at the intersection at Central Park West and 72nd Street outside the Dakota. Three acres of parkland, where he often walked, have been set aside in tribute to Lennon. It will be called Strawberry Fields.

Above: Later 100,000 mourners filled the Mall area (under the trees to the left) for a 10-minute, "Vigil of Silence" to John Lennon. There was an unusual golden glow in the air that day.

"Aurora Borealis"   1982

Gray and peach clouds   1982

Sheepskin clouds   1979

Clouds over upper 5th Avenue   1978

After the storm   1978

Orange sunrise   1979

RESODDING THE MEADOW

Above: Sheep Meadow as it looked before the lawn was worn out by heavy use . . . and the Tavern before extensive remodelling.   1959

Right: This crowd had gathered for one of the last New York Philharmonic concerts presented in the Meadow in 1979, and was the largest crowd I've ever photographed in the park. Over the years, the Meadow had become badly worn as the result of excessive use, not only from concerts, but from sports such as soccer, football, baseball and volleyball. That same summer the James Taylor concert raised $100,000 toward resodding the Meadow from the sale of T-shirts, buttons and from donations. One button pictured a bright green sheep saying "Keep the Sheep Meadow Green—The James Taylor Concert—July 13, 1979."

Left: By 1978 there were only a few patches of green lawn left on the Meadow. It was fascinating to watch what happened next. With enough money raised for its resodding—$400,000 from the state, $100,000 from the city and $100,000 from the Taylor concert—the Meadow was officially fenced off and closed in September 1979. First, drainage and irrigation pipes were laid out underground, and then the Meadow was regraded with new topsoil. For weeks all I saw from my window were hills of dirt being moved around and hundreds of yellow bags of peat moss scattered everywhere.   1979

Above: Then in April came all the yellow tractors—as fifteen acres of new green sod was unrolled. What a Midwestern scene to be going on right in the middle of Manhattan!   1979

Left: "An Italian hilltown." The fences were windbreaks to protect the newly planted sod. The Meadow was closed throughout the winter of 1979–80; we couldn't believe the parks department would keep everyone out for so long—but they did. Building the chain-link fence helped.   1980

Below: It was worth the wait. The Meadow officially reopened in August 1980. Today there are no sports, no concert crowds and no dogs on the Meadow. It's a lovely, protected spot with signs reading "This area is reserved for quiet recreation. Enjoy strolling, picnicking, kite flying, sunbathing. For hours, see a Ranger. No dogs please."   1981

On a sunny day   1982

At sunset   1982

Red buildings on
5th Avenue   1980

Early arrivals, a father and his two children   1959

Late arrivals   1977

Top: Olive Oyl, the first female float   1982

Bottom: The movie cast of "Annie"—Aileen Quinn, Geoffrey Holder, Albert Finney and Sandy—riding atop a float   1981

Right: Mickey Mouse walking down Central Park West   1981

134

The Tift County
Marching Band
from Tifton,
Georgia   1981

Spring 1967

So many things happen in the park that can't be seen from the street. Here is a fifty-foot geodesic dome that stood in the parking lot for five days as a display area for a fabric manufacturer. Watching the men build it was like watching circus performers.   1969

Warner Leroy reopened the Tavern on October 6, 1976, after it had been closed for two years. The ceremonies included a hot-air balloon from Great Adventure and an enormous ice cream "sundae" made of dozens of gallons of ice cream. Later it was entered into the *Guinness Book of World Records* as the world's largest, single ice cream sundae.

Left top: Dog obedience class   1975

Left bottom: Before the Tavern's reopening,
the parking lot was frequently used for publicity
purposes. Now, since the Tavern's seating
capacity has been enlarged, the parking lot is
usually filled with cars.   1975

Treasure hunt in a taxi. After a businessmen's
luncheon at the Tavern, the participants were
given a list of items that was apparently to be
gathered by taxi.   1963

White police vans   1975

"Star Wars" in mid-Manhattan   1983

Right: Three new towers—IBM, AT&T
and Trump Tower   1983

Left: "Save the Whale" rally   1979

Below: Buried balloon   1976

Balloons signal
the start of the
Women's 10km L'eggs
Mini Marathon   1982

144